Seriously Funny is Simon Brett's hundredth published book. Many of the previous ninety-nine are crime novels, including the Charles Paris, Mrs Pargeter, Fethering and Blotto & Twinks series. His humorous books include the best-selling *How To Be A Little Sod*. Work for radio and television includes the comedy series *After Henry* and *No Commitments*. Simon was educated at Dulwich College and Wadham College, Oxford, where he gained a First Class Honours Degree in English. A former radio and television producer, he has been a full-time writer since 1979. He was Chairman of the Crime Writers Association from 1986 to 1987 and of the Society of Authors from 1995 to 1997. In 2014 he was awarded the CWA Diamond Dagger 'for Excellence', and he was President of the Detection Club from 2001 to 2015. In the 2016 New Year's Honours he was awarded an OBE 'for services to literature'. He lives near Arundel in West Sussex and is married with three grown-up children, three grandsons, three granddaughters and three cats called Polly, Gordon and Gus.

Seriously

Funny
and Other Oxymorons

Simon Brett

with illustrations by Paul Thomas

ROBINSON

ROBINSON

First published in Great Britain in
2017 by Robinson

1 2 3 4 5 6 7 8 9 10

Text copyright © Simon Brett, 2017

Images © Paul Thomas, 2017

The moral right of the author has
been asserted.

A CIP catalogue record for this book
is available from the British Library.

ISBN: 978-1-47213-943-6

Designed by Andrew Barron
Typeset in Sentinel
Printed and bound in Great Britain
by Clays Ltd, St Ives plc

Papers used by Robinson are from
well-managed forests and other
responsible sources.

MIX
Paper from
responsible sources
FSC® C104740

Robinson
An imprint of
Little, Brown Book Group
Carmelite House
50 Victoria Embankment
London EC4Y 0DZ

An Hachette UK Company
www.hachette.co.uk

www.littlebrown.co.uk

To Ruth,
who's awfully good with words

—

Contents

General Specifics

As we all know, the Oxymoron is one of the undiscovered beauties of the English Language. It has been defined as 'a figure of speech that juxtaposes elements that appear to be contradictory'. Famous examples would include 'Bitter Sweet', 'Definite Maybe' and 'Compassionate Conservatism'.

A lot of the time we use Oxymorons without thinking. Some are so common that they've become part of everyday language. When we speak of acting naturally... or buy a medium-large garment... or say someone's pretty ugly...

the oxymoronic nature of the expressions is
probably not uppermost in our minds. But it's
there all right, hidden in plain sight (ooh, there's
another one!).

And you'll find a lot more examples, as you
read through *Seriously Funny*. So go on, if you
think you're going to have a devilishly good
(Oxymoron Alert!) time reading it, you're almost
exactly right (Oxymoron Alert!). Countless
numbers (Oxymoron Alert!) of you may even
scream with laughter (Oxymoron Alert!).
Hope so.

1

Home

Home
Comforts

The home should be a place of safety, a refuge from the challenges and difficulties of life in the big bad world. But it never quite works out like that. Owning or renting a home brings with it a whole raft of responsibilities. Domestic life is too often dominated by the demands of shopping and feeding people. And that's never easy, because these days when you get to the shops you're spoiled by too much choice. Then there are decisions to be made about how you decorate your home, how you want your garden to look, what kind of car you drive. And that's before you start thinking about your home's energy efficiency. It's a full-time job, just living. And if you're bringing up a family, the difficulties can be even greater . . . as spelled out in the following Oxymorons:

Alcohol-Free *Wine*

This seems rather to lose the point of wine. It tastes nothing like the real thing. People who don't want to drink alcohol should opt for other soft drinks rather than quaff this inadequate substitute.

___

Authentic *Replica*

An offer advertised in the back of colour supplements, which invites the purchaser to invest in something like medallions to commemorate 'Winston Churchill's Finest Hours (with free display case)'. They are frequently described as 'not only an enviable addition to your home décor, but also a solid investment'. Both claims are untrue.

___

Baby *Grand*

A small piano, as immortalised in the newspaper small ad: *'FOR SALE – Upright piano – owner getting grand.'*

———

Bag for *Life*

A carrier bag purchased on every visit to the supermarket (because you've always forgotten to take one of the other many Bags for Life you have hanging up in your kitchen).

———

Buy One *Get One Free*

6 This is an Oxymoron because of its ambiguous use of the word 'Free'. Commonly known as 'BOGOF', it's a promotional device from supermarkets whose aim is to encourage obesity and add to the fifteen million tonnes of food wasted in the UK every year.

——

Domestic *Bliss*

If only ...

——

Easy-to-Assemble
Furniture

The components delivered are never quite the same
as the pictures in the instructions. It is inevitable
that the Allen key will slip out of your fingers. The
advice: 'This part of the assembly will be more
easily done by two people' has broken up more
marriages than adultery.

———

Easy-to-Open
Food Packaging

*This has been the cause of many sandwich fillings
scattered across the room and much spillage of fruit
juice on to shirt fronts.*

———

Family *Entertainment*

8 The ideal of the whole family gathering round the single communal television to watch something which entertains them all is long gone. Nowadays a more likely scenario is the mother watching something about nuns and placentas on the television, the father watching sport on his laptop and the children watching porn on their tablets or phones.

Family *Meals*

The ideal of the whole family sitting round the communal dining table to eat a meal and enjoy sparkling conversation is now very rare. Most meals are consumed individually off laps in front of the television. And conversation is usually limited to: 'Ssh! I'm watching this.'

Foolproof *Instructions*

Self-assembly furniture items that come with these simply underestimate the foolishness of the fools that they're dealing with.

———

Free Gift *with Purchase*

Anyone foolish enough to think this means they're getting something for nothing is clearly untutored in the ways of the retail trade.

———

Fresh from *Concentrate*

Fruit juice concentrate is made by freezing and removing the water content from the squeezed juice for ease of transportation. It is then re-bulked by the addition of water. Which means it's a long way from being fresh.

——

Fuel *Economy*

Something promised in new cars, but never quite achieved.

——

Harmonious
House Purchase

There are no happy stories related to house
purchase. Perhaps it's because most people are
dealing with more money than at any other stage of
their life that they behave so badly. The possibility
of squeezing another five grand out of someone
destroys their moral compass. 'Chains', gazumping
and the taking on of huge debts cause a great deal of
stress, and the discomfort is exacerbated by having
to deal with estate agents. Every other country
in the world has a better system of purchasing
property than the English one.

———

Ill *Health*

*A lot of people suffer from this, and go on about it
at inordinate length. So, be very wary of using the
expression 'How are you?', because there are many
hypochondriacs out there who will tell you.*

———

Independent *Children*

12 Somehow, they never quite become independent. Because of the difficulties of getting on to the housing ladder, many return to live in the family home, just at the time their parents were thinking they might have a bit of time to do their own things. And even if the children set up in their own establishments, as the old Irish saying puts it, 'They leave your home but not your wallet.'

———

Moderate *Drinker*

This is the most common lie to be heard in doctors' surgeries, when the patient is asked to describe his or her relationship with alcohol.

———

Loyal *Cat*

A cat is loyal to whoever's putting out the
cat food.

———

Numb *Feeling*

*This can be prompted by many domestic events, such
as opening a spouse's credit card statement, picking
up the telephone bill for a teenager in love, or simply
standing on the bathroom scales.*

———

Odourless *Cat Litter*

Whatever it may say on the packaging, once
a cat's used it, there is no such thing.

———

Odourless *Dog*

Again, there is no such thing. Dogs smell, full stop. And they smell even worse when it's been raining.

——

Reliable *Sat Nav*

Though pretty good at getting a driver roughly to where he or she's going, Sat Navs often fail to pinpoint the exact spot being aimed for. The result is a lot of driving back and forth on dark country lanes.

——

Rubber *Cement*

Ideal for people who bounce off the walls.

——

Sale *Bargain*

Always remember that retailers are not Fairy Godmothers. If something's in a sale, it's because it's outdated stock which the shopkeeper can't get rid of at a higher price.

——

Sleeping *Like a Baby*

People who use this expression to mean 'sleeping peacefully' have clearly never had a baby.

——

Trusted *Car Dealers*

If only ...

———

Vegetarian *Meatball*

This is one of many Oxymorons in the world of food. Almost every meat product seems to be available in a vegetarian version. You'd think people would be more inventive in naming things.

———

Waterproof *Sponge*

This would seem to defeat the purpose of something that was created to mop up water.

———

2

Political
Principles

Politicians spend much of their lives using doublespeak, making statements which they instantly contradict, so Oxymorons provide a perfect means of communication for them. As George Orwell put it, 'In our time, political speech and writing are largely the defence of the indefensible … Thus, political language has to consist largely of euphemism, question-begging and sheer cloudy vagueness.' How well Oxymorons fit into this world. They are perfect labour-saving devices for politicians, whose lives are spent trying to avoid giving direct answers to direct questions. Wonderfully, Oxymorons enable them to express two opposing points of view within a single phrase. No wonder they are so frequently used in Parliament.

Here are some favourites from the political world:

Affordable *Housing*

This is something that politicians are always talking about but never producing. For anyone who lives in London the concept is laughable.

———

Big *Society*

This was an initiative introduced by former Prime Minister David Cameron. Its aim was to encourage volunteers to fill in some of the deficiencies in local services caused by government cutbacks. It didn't work because it failed to take into account the basic selfishness of the human race and the fact that most societies are very small-minded.

———

Blind *Eye*

An essential physical attribute for any politician.
Every day there are more things towards which
it must be turned. The expression is said to have
originated at the Battle of Copenhagen in 1801,
when Admiral Nelson was sent a signal from his
pussy-footed superior Admiral Sir Hyde Parker to
discontinue the attack. Nelson put his telescope
to his blind eye, looked in the direction where the
relevant flags conveying the message were flying,
and said, 'I really do not see the signal.' The result
was the disgrace of Sir Hyde Parker and Nelson's
appointment as Commander-in-Chief.

———

Calculated *Error*

24

Very handy for politicians. If they make a cock-up whose results, through no efforts of their own, turn out to be beneficial, they claim it as a 'Calculated Error'.

___

Campaign *Promises*

Much is made of these during election campaigns. Post-election they are all conveniently forgotten.

___

Civil *Servant*

Anyone who has dealt with such bureaucrats   **25**
knows that they are rarely civil. Their attitude to
their work is summed up in this question from a
(fictitious) Civil Service Entrance Exam:

'If you are about to take your lunchbreak and a
female member of the general public comes to you
with an enquiry, you should address her in which of
the following ways?

1   Can I assist you, Madam?
2   Can I assist you, Miss?
3   Can I assist you, Ms?
4   Wow, gorgeous! Are you free this evening?

The correct answer is: None of the above. If you
are about to take your lunchbreak, you ignore her
completely.'

———

Committee *Decision*

Committees are not famed for reaching any decisions, nor, when they do, making good ones. This is summed up in the famous line: 'A camel is a horse designed by a committee.' The usual response of a committee to making a difficult decision is to appoint a sub-committee to investigate the possibilities.

———

Community *Care*

This policy, also known as 'Care in the Community', involved closing down large institutions for those with special needs and having them looked after in their own homes. As with most government initiatives, it was in fact a cost-cutting exercise, which failed because there were not enough professional carers to look after the disadvantaged. Basically, the Community did not Care.

———

Compassionate *Conservatism*

You gotta be joking.

———

Conviction *Politician*

This means either:

A A politician who tries to get elected on the premise that he believes in something.

B A politician with a criminal record.

Neither is to be trusted.

———

Criminal *Justice*

The only kind available.

——

Government *Efficiency*

The checks and balances within government systems make it very difficult to get anything done quickly. The only thing that governments are efficient at is generating mounds of redundant paperwork. The situation can be summed up in the old saying: 'An elephant is a mouse designed to government specifications.'

——

Government *Initiative*

A plan which is announced with a huge flourish and which never gets implemented.

———

Great *Britain*

In the days of the British Empire (a huge amount of territory run from a relatively tiny geographical hub) this expression had some validity. More recent events – and particularly very recent events – have reduced Britain to a status more commensurate with its size. The Falklands War was probably the last twitch of the dying Empire's tail, and that didn't do anyone much good . . . except for Margaret Thatcher, whom it got re-elected.

———

Local Government *Worker*

Local government is not a sector which always attracts the brightest of employees, as illustrated by this story:

'A man parked his car and noticed two men working by the side of the road. The first was digging holes and the second was filling them in. Having watched this process a couple of times, the man was curious and asked them what they were doing.

The hole-digger replied, "We work for the local council. Normally, we're a three-man team. I dig the hole, Fred puts the tree in, and Pete here fills in the hole. Just because Fred's off sick today, that doesn't mean Pete and I can't do our jobs."'

——

Manifesto *Promises*

See Campaign Promises.

——

New *Labour*

This concept, introduced by Tony Blair in 1994, was in fact Old Conservatism.

———

Private *Email*

Not any more.

———

Retrospective *Planning*

Bizarre though it may sound, in the world of building regulations, retrospective planning is a common occurrence. But it's an Oxymoron that could apply to a great many areas of government policy where post-cock-up decisions have to be justified.

———

Soft *Brexit*

A meaningless expression. Achieving any kind of Brexit is going to be extremely hard.

—

Titanic *Success*

This is what Boris Johnson claimed the UK would make of Brexit. He could be right about the 'Titanic' bit.

—

Trump *Diplomacy*

Trump Diplomacy

—

Young *Conservative*

There is a political trend observable in many human beings. The idealism of youth tends to favour Left Wing views; with the cynicism of age, Right Wing views take over. To put it more simply, young people who don't possess anything naturally embrace Socialism, a creed which believes that property should be spread more evenly. They are also appalled by the greed and cynicism of the Conservatives. When they grow older and possess money and property they become Conservative (there is a clue in the word) because they want to conserve their possessions and not let them get into the hands of all those thieving Socialists. For this reason, Young Conservatives are usually people who have inherited something. As the old saying goes, 'It is good to save money, but it's better if your parents did it for you.'

A Party Political Broadcast
on behalf of
the Oxymoron Party

———

(though actually it could be any other party)

34   Good evening. We in the Oxymoron Party believe in clean politics. We believe exclusively in a big tent approach to public service. We advocate toeing an independent party line, finding more flexible rigidity in the justice system, and championing minority rights for all. We believe in public-private partnerships. In a word, we are in favour of simple politics, conducted by simple politicians. We are immovable in our desire for change, and our hidden agenda is to achieve transparency.

So, let us consider some broad-brush details of the Oxymoron Party's policies. In matters of foreign affairs, we are looking for grassroots internationalism. In matters of industrial relations, we are looking for an open-door policy on closed shops. In matters of race, we are looking for a more diverse integrity. In matters of security, we are prepared to take risks.

While the other parties offer unfulfilled promises, we in the Oxymoron Party deal in definite possibilities. When we are in government, we will set up a new department to minimise bureaucracy. We will ring-fence free access to foreign markets. We will control entrepreneurship. We will listen to the voice of the Silent Majority. We will put the 'Great' back into 'Britain'. Above all, we will provide a caring government, whose relaxed authority will bring untold benefits to all voters – man, woman and child.

So, vote Oxymoron. We are the party of political optimism. As we look nostalgically through the mists of the future, we see brightness ahead.

———

3

Business
Ethics

The commercial world is based on the 39
principle of making a profit, and over the
centuries there have always been entrepreneurs
not too fussy about how that profit was made.
Ethics just don't come into the equation, and
we live in an age when bankers are reckoned to
have less integrity than estate agents or even
politicians. As a result, business dealings and
financial transactions are now, as they always
have been, open to finagling and duplicity.
This is obviously a rich seam to be mined for
Oxymorons, of which the following are examples:

Bad *Credit*

'Credit' is, by definition, something good.
People who have 'bad credit' are vulnerable
to advertisements from the shysters who
call themselves Pay-Day Loan Companies.
These typically have an interest rate of 1295%
Representative APR.

Banking *Integrity*

*A nostalgic phrase, recalling something that no
longer exists.*

British *Manufacturing Industry*

See Banking Integrity.

Corporate *Planning*

See Retrospective Planning **(Political Principles).** 41

———

Easy *Money*

Getting money is never easy.

———

Easy *Payments*

Paying for things is never easy.

———

Easy *Terms*

See Easy Payments.

———

Farewell *Reception*

This is an event to celebrate the retirement of a member of staff. The usual format is a lot of drink followed by a speech from a senior executive, who is meeting the retiree for the first time. Reading from notes prepared by his P.A., the executive waxes fulsome about what a good company person the retiree has always been, how much he will be missed and how he will now have more time to enjoy his hobbies (ignoring the fact that he's been worked so hard he's never had time to develop any hobbies).

Filing *System*

Filing systems are as various as the people who use them. The arrival of computers was supposed to have revolutionised the operation, replacing scraps of paper and card with digital records. The average office worker is still capable of making it impossible to find files.

Flexible *Finance*

Whatever words are used to dress it up, the fact 43
remains that at some point bills have to be paid in full.

────

Free *Market*

The word 'market' is defined as 'a place where
commodities are bought and sold'. So, the idea of a
'free market' . . . in your dreams.

────

Honest *Broker*

This expression was coined by Otto von Bismarck
(in German, of course) to describe his role in the 1878
Congress of Berlin. It would not be used by anyone
who has ever had dealings with a stockbroker.

────

Job *Security*

A distant memory.

——

Paper-Free *Office*

The advent of computers was supposed to cut down the amount of paper in offices. The trouble is that computers also made it easy to generate huge volumes of hard copies of every digital document and there are still workers who don't quite trust the new technology and make copies of everything 'just to be sure'. The result is an increase in the amount of paper which litters many offices.

——

Risk-Free *Investment*

There is no such thing as a risk-free investment.

——

Safe *Bet*

There is no such thing as a safe bet.

———

Secure *Pension*

There is no such thing as a secure pension.

———

Semi-Retired

People who describe themselves as this are really retired. Their responsibilities have been taken over by younger employees, but they like to maintain the illusion of usefulness. Some still put in occasional appearances at their place of work, like the retired gynaecologist who still worked one day a week because he liked to keep his hand in.

———

Understanding
Bank Manager

Those days are gone.

Victimless *Crime*

46 There is a prevalent – and rather comforting – view
that offences like fiddling expenses or cheating
insurance companies are victimless crimes
because they are done at the expense of monolithic
corporations rather than of individual people.
The boring truth is that individuals do suffer from
restricted pay rises or increased premiums caused
by such actions.

Working *Breakfast*

*A tradition established by people who want to
impress their clients and colleagues by being so busy
that they can't even let breakfast be separate from the
rest of the working day. Such people lack the skill of
time management.*

4

Enduring
Fashion

Following fashion is one of the most illogical, but also deeply engrained, of human behaviours. Few of us can truly say that we are indifferent to fashion – though we may not take it to its most extreme level. Maybe the impulse is a product of basic insecurity. People who don't feel adequate in themselves look up to those who seem to stride through the world with confidence, and hope that, by copying their appearance and habits, some of that confidence will rub off. The inadequate are, of course, destined for lives of constant disappointment. Why is it that a garment, when brought home and put on, never looks as good as it did in the shop?

Whatever the reasons, the reach of fashion – be it in clothes, décor or the latest fitness fad – is very hard to escape. And its constant desire for change and redefinition gives rise to many Oxymorons, of which the following are examples:

Balding *Hair*

52 A common affliction, particularly for men. It brings
to mind the old aphorism: 'Experience is the comb
that life gives you when you have lost your hair.'

———

Comfortable *High Heels*

*It is a source of wonder and admiration among men
that women are prepared to endure the constant pain
of fashionable footwear. One has only to look at the
number of plasters on the women's heels to begin to
understand the agonies they go through.*

———

Designer *Jeans*

The development of durable working garments into overpriced designer items is characteristic of the fashion industry. The fad for making the fabric less durable by 'distressing' or sandblasting is another example of silliness. And ripping open the knees of perfectly good pairs of jeans

A   looks terrible, and
B   is plain daft, and
C   cold.

—

Fake *Tan*

Popular with television presenters who want to look orange.

—

53

Fashionable *Flip-Flops*

No such thing. Though very practical and comfortable, Flip-Flops always look terrible.

———

Fashionable *Socks*

See Fashionable Flip-Flops.

———

Healthy *Tan*

Tans may look good, but modern science knows that they are caused by harmful ultraviolet radiation. If you have a tan, achieved by exposure to the sun or in a tanning salon, you've sustained skin cell damage. Which can lead to wrinkles, brown spots and skin cancer. If this makes you feel that you should resort to *Fake Tan* (q.v.), that also has its drawbacks.

———

Jolie Laide

This is a French term to describe someone who, without being conventionally pretty, is still very attractive. It is one of those things French women can carry off. Somehow, the English translation, 'Pretty Ugly', doesn't hack it in quite the same way.

———

Lingerie *Model*

A woman married to a footballer.

———

Long *Shorts*

Every length of shorts has been experimented with
at some point, and the clothes industry has tried,
without marked success, to make every length
fashionable. What they don't take into account
is the fact that how shorts look depends on the
legs of the wearer, and at least fifty per cent of the
population should never be seen dead in them.

———

Loose *Tights*

Uncomfortable.

———

Natural *Hair Dye for Men*

You can always tell when men's hair has been dyed.

———

Natural *Hair Extensions*

The only natural way of extending one's hair is by letting it grow.

———

One Size *Fits All*

Maybe, but it doesn't fit them all equally well.

———

Shabby *Chic*

Overpriced.

———

Smart *Baseball Cap*

The Baseball Cap has swept through society rather in the manner of the Black Death. It is equally unattractive. Everyone who wears a baseball cap would look better not wearing it.

———

Smart *Casual*

If you see this dress code on an invitation, it means you can wear anything – or nothing.

———

Tight *Slacks*

See Loose Tights.

———

Undetectable *Toupé*

No such thing. Toupés always look like toupés
and it is a source of enduring puzzlement why
anyone would ever wear one. Also, how do wearers
announce their sudden regrowth of hair? It must
be very difficult when a bald office worker walks in
one day with what looks like a piece of roadkill or
Shredded Wheat on his head. Is it appropriate for
his colleagues to comment on the transformation?
Sadly, no etiquette books seem to provide answers
to this ticklish problem.

———

5

Military
Intelligence

The history of the incompetence of armies is as old as warfare itself. Training men to 'answer orders at all times without question' was never going to do much for their intellectual development. And having those orders given by people appointed for their social status rather than their competence was hardly likely to help the situation.

Because of this background, warfare has always been a great breeding ground for Oxymorons. As a headline in the *Daily Herald* during the Second World War put it:

WAR OFFICE ADMITS OFFICERS
NEED INTELLIGENCE

Here are some examples of military Oxymorons:

Arms *Limitation*

A system whereby countries with huge stockpiles of arms prevent countries with smaller stockpiles of arms from making them any bigger.

Civil *War*

No war has ever been civil and, generally speaking, internal wars between factions within a single country have been bloodier and with longer-lasting repercussions than wars between separate nations.

Defensive *Strike*

This is the basic principle of getting your retaliation in first, favoured since time immemorial by playground bullies.

Enemy *Within*

As well as referring to home-grown terrorists, this expression can also apply to enemies within the institution of the army. The French philosopher Helvétius wrote that 'discipline is simply the art of making the soldiers fear their officers more than the enemy'. Or, as Aubrey Menen put it, 'It is the man who is afraid of the *enemy's* General Staff that is a coward; the man who is afraid of his own is merely an old soldier.' The Duke of Wellington's opinion of his troops is well known: 'I don't know what effect these men will have upon the enemy, but, by God, they frighten me.'

———

Enhanced *Interrogation*

An ugly expression used by the American military.
It is a euphemism for torture. Initiated under the
Presidency of George W. Bush, it was used in various
'black sites' around the world, including Abu Ghraib
and Guantanamo Bay. In July 2014, the European
Court ruled that 'enhanced interrogation' is definitely
torture. But such niceties are not likely to bother
President Trump.

Friendly *Fire*

Managing at the same time to be both an Oxymoron and a euphemism, this is also one of the cruellest expressions in the military world. Killing your own troops unfortunately has a long history in warfare. Less likely to happen in the days when soldiers wielded swords, spears and axes – though arrows could easily get misdirected – such incidents became much more common with the development of mechanised **warfare.**

Perhaps one of the most famous people to suffer from this kind of death was Robert Pierrepont, First Earl of Kingston-upon-Hull. Neutral at the beginning of the English Civil War, he made what

was to prove to be an unfortunately prophetic remark: 'When ... I take arms with the King against Parliament, or with the Parliament against the King, let a cannonball divide me between them.' He later sided with the King and became Lieutenant-General of the Royalist army in East Anglia. Unfortunately, in the defence of the Lincolnshire town of Gainsborough, he was taken captive by the Parliamentarians. On 25 July 1643, he was in a boat on the way to Hull, guarded by his enemies, when Royalist soldiers decided to shoot at his captors. Sadly, one of their cannonballs neatly bisected their own commander, Robert Pierrepont. Oops!

Glorious *Defeat*

72 Military history offers many examples of this Oxymoron. The Charge of the Light Brigade, which took place on 25 October 1854 during the Crimean War, fits the bill. Due to the wrong command being given, around six hundred and eighty cavalrymen attacked Russian gun emplacements. One hundred and eighteen men were killed, one hundred and twenty-seven wounded, and some sixty taken prisoner. Though, according to Tennyson's famous poem, 'Someone had blunder'd', remarkably this glorious defeat served to enhance the reputation of the cavalrymen. Nearly a century later, the Evacuation of Dunkirk, a retreat by any definition, was hailed as a great triumph. Former American President Richard M. Nixon had some words of wisdom on the subject: 'You've got to learn to survive a defeat. That's when you develop character.' Sadly for him, the character he developed was not enough to prevent his being impeached and removed from office.

Holy *Wars*

Wars conducted in the name of various religions have never involved less brutality and bloodshed than wars which followed the more honestly claimed motives of greed, revenge, acquisition of territory and power-grabbing. In 1095 Pope Urban II, starting the First Crusade, declaimed, 'When an armed attack is made upon the enemy, let this one cry be raised by all the soldiers of God: "It is the will of God! It is the will of God!"' He then, rather conveniently, absolved all crusaders of all their sins, giving another motive for the ensuing carnage.

Limited *Airstrike*

See Precision Bombing.

Lovable *Squaddie*

There are no lovable squaddies.

———

Loyal *Mercenary*

Soldiers working for personal gain rather than ideological motives have been around as long as war itself. They were certainly used in the thirteenth century BC by Rameses II. They have always been available to the highest bidder and therefore frequently change sides.

———

Militant *Pacifist*

'I am not only a pacifist but a militant pacifist. I am willing to fight for peace. Nothing will end war unless the people themselves refuse to go to war.' Those words are from Albert Einstein, who knew a thing or two about things. And, of course, pacifist principles are frequently challenged. It's very difficult always to turn the other cheek. One of the tenets of the Quaker religion is a refusal to participate in war or any other kind of violence. But there are ways round the principle, as this story demonstrates:

'A devout Quakeress lived in the country with her husband. She woke up to the sound of something breaking downstairs. She woke her husband. "Samuel, listen. I think there's a prowler. Thee needs to go see." The Quaker got up, grabbed a hunting rifle and just as he came to the top of the stairs, sure enough, there was the prowler opposite him below, frozen at the sight of a gun pointed at him. The Quaker, aiming the gun right at the man said: "Friend, I mean thee no harm, but thou art standing where I am about to shoot."'

———

Officer *Class*

Officers rarely have much class, and have been vilified throughout history for poor decision-making. As the eighteenth-century wit Lord Chesterfield said of the generals of his day, 'I only hope that when the enemy reads the list of their names, he trembles as I do.' The British infantry of the First World War were famously described as 'lions led by donkeys', and there is a long tradition of 'donkeys' in the military high command. Nor was the route into the Officer Class always one of choice. As Edward Ward wrote in his 1709 book, *Mars Stript of His Armour, or The Army Described in All Its True Colours*: 'An ensign's usually a young gentleman who passed through all the classes of his education handsomely enough and was ripe for the university, being designed for a clergyman; but unfortunately happening to be caught abed with one of his mother's chambermaids, the scene was changed and the young spark was doomed to the army.'

Peacekeeping *Mission*

War by another name.

———

Precision *Bombing*

In theory, the advanced sophistication of targeting technology means that a bomb can find and take out a single building. In practice – when, as is not always the case, the right building has been targeted – adjacent structures are also destroyed, almost always with the loss of civilian lives. Precision bombing works on the principle of treating a corn on the toe by amputating the whole leg.

———

Safety *Weapons*

No weapons are safe; that's why they're called weapons, dangerous to friend and foe alike. As the old schoolboy howler put it: 'If his rifle fails, the British soldier always has the good old bayonet to fall back on.'

——

Security *Risk*

Soldiers should always be on guard against breaches of security. They cannot be too careful. As one veteran put it: 'In my regiment we used to shoot first and ask questions afterwards. Of course, we never got many answers.'

——

War *Game*

In theory, this describes a training exercise. In
practice, throughout history too many military
commanders have regarded war as a game, with
the horrendous casualties to prove it. 'The Great
Game', which filled most of the nineteenth century,
was a conflict between the British Empire and
the Russian Empire over the fate of Central Asia.
In spite of its name, the Great Game managed to
include a lot of wars.

79

———

6

Practical

Religion

82 Churchgoing in the United Kingdom has been in decline for a long time. If attendance is the measure of such things, then the British live in one of the most godless countries on earth. And yet many people still, if asked to state their religion on a form, put 'C of E' (except of course for those who put 'Jedi', 'Wiccan' or 'Tree-Worshipper', but they do tend just to be exhibitionists).

There are any number of belief systems in the world, ranging from the highly organised to the frankly flakey. Most of us, in this secular age, aren't too bothered what others believe in, so long as it doesn't involve killing people. But within religious groups there can be a fierce resistance to members of other faiths. The individual believers can have the strong conviction that they alone are right, they are convinced that they alone will have a free run of heaven, and some can even take great delight in thinking of all those outside their creed who will be cast into everlasting darkness.

Because of the inherent conflicts within belief systems, they offer lots of Oxymorons.

Accurate *Horoscopes*

84 Yet to be invented. Astonishing, though, how many people, while dismissing the concept as 'superstitious nonsense', still go quickly to the relevant page in the newspaper to read how their day is not going to turn out. In the words of Isaac Asimov, 'I don't believe in astrology; I'm a Sagittarius and we're sceptical.'

———

Anglican *Fundamentalist*

The Church of England is a social institution, whose sole aim is to make people who like singing carols feel good at Christmas. The idea that it should involve passionate commitment to any belief system would be mildly distasteful to most members of its congregation – and certainly confuse its clergy.

———

Catholic *Truth*

Catholic authorities have always been very good at redefining what constitutes truth. The basic tenet of Catholicism has always been that its adherents believe what the Catholic hierarchy tells them to believe. There are many other religions which follow this principle, but few of them do it as efficiently as the Catholics.

——

Charismatic *Christianity*

However much you try to jazz them up, most religious rites remain dull and repetitive.

——

Christian *Charity*

Not always in evidence. Just listen to the views of
ladies who do the church flowers about the other
ladies on the church flowers rota.

Christian *Pagan*

Someone who wants to have it both ways.

Devout *Atheist*

Most people in this category once had a strong
faith. They take the same fervency with which they
used to support religion into their attacks on it.
They have this in common with reformed drinkers,
smokers and divorcees. As the old epigram has it,
'Anyone who breaks a habit generally frames the
pieces.'

Doubtful *Belief*

See Religious Scepticism.

___

False *Prophet*

History provides many examples of men – and
sometimes women – who used the claims of
divine inspiration to lead people astray. It's one
of the oldest cons in the book, and still prevalent.
Hardly a year goes by without some American
television evangelist being found to have pocketed
all the money pledged by innocent believers to his
church. Beware of such people – particularly the
anonymous one who coined the line: 'There is no
God and I am his prophet.'

___

Good *Samaritan*

Because the Jews of biblical times despised the Samaritans and believed all kinds of evil of them, the expression 'Good Samaritan' would be regarded by them as an Oxymoron. Jesus's parable of the Samaritan who helps a man who's been mugged was designed to demonstrate the importance of ethical behaviour over religious formalism. A modern version of the parable goes like this:

'A certain man went down from Jerusalem and Jericho, and he was set upon by a thief, which stripped him of his raiment, and wounded him, and departed, leaving him half dead. And by chance there came down a certain priest that way: and when he saw him, he passed by on the other side. And likewise a Levite, when he was at the place, came and looked on him, and passed by on the other side. But two psychiatrists, as they journeyed, came where he was, and when they saw him, bloody and bruised, one said to the other, "We must find the person who did this. He needs help!"'

New English *Bible*

A version of the holy text written by people with tin ears. They must have gone through the entire text of the King James Bible and, whenever they heard a phrase with rhythm, cadence or beauty, replaced it with something flat and unmusical.

———

New Revised *Standard Version*

See New English Bible.

———

Rational *Faith*

Many great thinkers have tried – and failed – to rationalise faith. The fact is that faith is stronger than reason, and therein lies its beauty. As that very great thinker Anon put it, 'Religion is like a blind man looking in a black room for a black cat that isn't there, and finding it.'

———

Religious *Scepticism*

The creation of the first god coincided with the creation of the first person who didn't believe he (or she) was for real. And the strength of belief has always varied according to what one is being asked to believe in. As the American comedian George Carlin put it, 'Tell people there's an invisible man in the sky who created the universe, and the vast majority will believe you. Tell them the paint is wet, and they have to touch it to be sure.'

———

Religious *Toleration*

No religion has a very good track record for tolerating other religions. Though ecumenism is much discussed and there are many initiatives to get different church traditions to communicate with each other, the true believer really does think his or her faith is the only one that's right. And they have a basic contempt for all the others. The point is made in the following story:

A man is shipwrecked on a desert island. Being of a practical nature, he makes himself tools, digs up rocks and cuts down trees to build himself somewhere to live. As the years pass, he puts up more and more buildings. Eventually, as always happens in stories about men shipwrecked on desert islands, a ship

arrives and its captain comes on shore to rescue him.
But the man on the island is not so worried about
rescue; he's more concerned to show the captain his
building work. The visitor is duly impressed by the
luxurious house and its many amenities, but when
he's taken out the back he is amazed by the sight of two
complete stone-built churches.

'What do you think of that?' asks the castaway.

'Brilliant,' says the captain, 'but tell me – why have
you built two of them?'

'Ah,' says the man, pointing as he speaks. 'That's
the one I go to.' He points at the other church. 'And
that's the one I don't go to.'

AN OXYMORONIC
SERMON

——

94   I take as my text today, from the much-read Book of Exodus, the Ninth Commandment: 'Thou shalt not bear false witness against thy neighbour.' And I welcome you all to the Church of the Holy Oxymoron, an exclusive sect that is open to all. Here, we glory in the church's long history of religious tolerance, offering a free-form ritual and a creed that you just will not believe!

Those who join the Church of the Holy Oxymoron find themselves within the confines of a broad church, which embraces religious liberalism. We do not reject the tenets of other agnostic faiths, like Christian Science, Guilt-free Catholicism or Charismatic Anglicanism. Above all, we believe in one-size-fits-all individualism, which enables each corporeal soul to enjoy the benefits of solitary communion.

The Church of the Holy Oxymoron has a widely
dispersed congregation. Our beliefs encompass
a grounded transcendentalism, which leads to
an immutable transformation of the individual
soul. For us, death is not the end, rather an
unsurpassable portal to an animated afterlife.
Then, at the end of a finite eternity, the false
witnesses will be cast into the flames of unending
darkness. Meanwhile those who are randomly
chosen will enjoy the unworldly benefits of
everlasting life, and will stand up and be counted
when they sit at the right hand of God.

This will be the fortuitous destiny of those who
join the Church of the Holy Oxymoron.

Praise be to God.

7 **User**

Technology

Friendly
Technology

In the last fifty years, our lives have been totally transformed by developments in Information Technology. Computers have taken over, hugely speeding up processes that used to have to move at the speed of the human brain. Mobile phones now join up the whole world, and not just by conversation. Social media allow people to send friends photos of their lunch the moment it's delivered. What more could we ask?

We don't need to know how all this technology works, but we do need to know how to fix it when something doesn't work. And the older we get, the more frustrating that becomes. There's the story of a mature new computer owner trying to set up his internet connection. After some hours of frustration, he rang a helpline, only to be told, 'It's so simple a five-year-old child could do it.' 'Well,' the owner snarled, 'fetch me a five-year-old child!'

The IT world, with its amazing turnover of highly vaunted new products, is a natural breeding-ground for Oxymorons. How many of us have read the instruction, 'To shut down, click the "Start" button', without thinking there's something odd about it? Here are a few more Oxymorons from the further reaches of technology:

Easy-to-Follow *Instructions*

They never are.

—

Essential *App*

Something you've managed perfectly well without all your life.

—

Fast *Download*

It rather depends on your definition of 'fast'.

101

———

Fast Free *Wi-Fi*

A lot of hotels claim to have this. They never do.

———

Interesting *Blog*

Blogs are the contemporary outlet for people who used to send newspapers letters in green ink with lots of underlinings in them. Writers of blogs are people overfond of the sound of their own voices. Fortunately, most of the blogs posted online are never read, thus saving the general public a great deal of time and aggravation.

———

Long *Battery Life*

This is an Oxymoron when applied to mobile phones. The battery life of all mobile phones is disappointingly short.

Online *Banking*

A simple, streamlined and efficient system enabling people to take your money without going to the bother of sourcing guns, stocking masks and getaway cars.

Online *Support*

See also *Useful FAQ. Online Support provides answers for all the technological problems except the one your equipment has got. As a result, you usually end up getting advice on a premium-rate phone line.*

Reliable *GPS*

GPS on smart phones is fairly reliable, but often fails to pinpoint the final destination (*See* Reliable Sat Nav, **Home Comforts**). As a result, particularly in urban areas, you get a lot of people striding up and down, looking with puzzlement at their phones, walking into other pedestrians and lampposts.

Smart *Phone*

A smart phone, sadly, is only as smart as the person using it. The really smart people, of course, are those who manufacture smart phones and ensure that their customers have to upgrade to a new model every few months.

Social *Media*

Communication systems which enable antisocial people to avoid the necessity of talking to each other.

Virtual *Reality*

Somewhere much more attractive than the real
thing ... though it is getting increasingly difficult to
tell the two apart.

———

Useful *FAQ*

*FAQ is an abbreviation for 'Frequently Asked
Questions'. Lists of FAQs are guaranteed to list the
answer to every question except the one you want the
answer to.*

———

Wi-Fi *Available*

This phrase appears in all brochures for foreign
holiday accommodation. It is never true.

———

8

Fair

Game

The leisure industry – and there's an Oxymoron for you – has always been organised and commercialised, and nowhere is that more true than in the world of sport. The Romans who watched gladiatorial combat in huge stadia were being bribed with 'bread and circuses' by their overlords. And from the start all sports were deeply involved with gambling. The Corinthian ideal of the altruistic athlete, who plays for the love of the game, was always a kind of myth. Later on, hunting, hawking and pig-sticking could only be afforded by the very rich.

It is no surprise then that sport has always proved to be a rich hunting-ground for Oxymorons.

Baseball *World Series*

Only the Americans could, without irony, call a contest between the American League and the National League champions a *World Series*.

——

English-Speaking *Premier League Footballer*

These are very rarely sighted.

——

FIFA *Ethics*

When it was announced that FIFA was to host a conference on ethics, the *Los Angeles Times* wrote: 'Think about that for a second: the global sports organisation most synonymous with corruption and obfuscation is holding a forum focused on morality and openness.' There has always been corruption in football, and its incidence has increased as the money involved in the sport has reached stratospheric levels. There is a kind of career progression in the ways of corruption. Footballers who earned massive salaries during their playing years try to maintain their high earnings in retirement by going into the administration of the sport. Bribery is as much a part of football as the ball itself.

———

Fitness *Injury*

This expression is all too commonly heard, as people who've never taken any exercise in their lives suddenly get blackmailed into going to the gym. Weights, treadmills and other fitness equipment are all potential hazards to the inexperienced. And a lot of people, while checking on their Fitbits how many steps they've taken, walk into lampposts.

———

Football, *'The Beautiful Game'*

Pelé is said to have coined this phrase. He'd clearly never watched a nil-nil draw in the rain. Or observed the antics of English football hooligans.

———

Golf *Fashion*

Golfers have the same level of fashion sense as Abba.

—

Good-Looking *Darts Player*

Watching darts on television is very encouraging for people who are low on the physical attraction spectrum. It shows that even the terminally ugly can get hordes of enthusiastic fans (including a lot of women) screaming at them in adoration.

———

Healthy *Competition*

The human desire to win can all too quickly turn healthy competition into unhealthy competition.

———

Interesting *Golfer*

These are very rarely sighted. Golfers are all
incredibly self-centred and can only talk about golf,
as is illustrated in the following story:

*'A golfer was in the golf club bar, taking his girlfriend
through every stroke of the round he had just
completed. After about three-quarters of an hour, he
said, "Anyway, enough about me. What did you think
of my bunker shot on the seventeenth?"'*

———

Light-*Heavyweight*

Make your bloody mind up!

———

Metal *Wood*

116 Heavy-headed golf clubs with long shafts, designed to hit the ball long distances, used to be made of wood, often persimmon. Now many of them are made of metal. This doesn't make much difference to the average amateur golfer who, whatever club he's using, can still be relied on to slice the ball into the rough. Which prompts a recollection of the following story:

'A man is playing golf and his caddie seems to be spending ages finding him the right club.

"Oh, for heaven's sake!" says the golfer. "You must be the worst caddie on earth!"

"I doubt it," says the caddie. "That would be too much of a coincidence."'

———

Olympic *Ideal*

To the Olympic motto, 'swifter, higher, stronger', should be added the word 'richer'. For the true Olympian, the ideal is to make as much money as possible.

——

Poor *Bookmaker*

There is no such thing as a poor bookmaker.

——

Rich *Punter*

For the only people who regularly make money out of gambling, it is not a hobby. They spend as long on their research and planning as they would if they were doing any other job. Though there are examples of lucky punters winning huge bets, most of them very quickly lose their winnings by trying to repeat the trick. As the old saying has it, 'The only way to end an afternoon's racing with a million pounds is by starting the day with ten million.'

Scrum *Rules*

In rugby there apparently are rules for what happens in the scrum, but nobody knows what they are.

Thrilling Day's *Cricket*

Cricket is the Marmite of sports. Its enthusiasts could use this expression without irony. Those who take the opposing view worry about the sanity of a country whose national game takes five days. And they probably share the view of Lord Mancroft: 'Cricket is a game which the British, not being a spiritual people, had to invent in order to have some concept of eternity.'

———

Woman *Batsman*

Traditional cricket commentators have never quite caught on to the idea of gender equality. Cricket remains the most misogynistic of sports. As Denis Norden put it, 'It's a funny kind of month, October. For the really keen cricket fan it's when you discover that your wife left you in May.'

———

9

Popular Culture

The line between one's working life and one's
time of relaxation has always been a wobbly
one. Noel Coward said that 'work is much more
fun than fun', and modern millennials constantly
agonise over their work/life balance. Now,
thanks to modern technology, we probably have
more access to entertainment than any other
preceding generation. But why is it, given so
many possibilities, we can so rarely find in the
listings a movie that we actually want to watch?
Or why, when browsing the titles in a bookshop,
can we so rarely find one we want to read? Spoilt
for choice perhaps? But then most people have
always had a certain ambivalence about the arts.
And ambivalence engenders Oxymorons:

Act *Naturally*

Actors are very bad at doing this when they're not onstage. And when one is onstage playing the part of an actor, he or she is more unbelievable than ever.

——

Critical *Acclaim*

What it really means is 'Uncritical Acclaim'.

——

Easy Listening *Richard Clayderman*

A matter of opinion.

——

Electric *Acoustic Guitar*

*This is now so much a part of a musician's
equipment that it is no longer thought of as an
Oxymoron.*

Female *Actor*

A politically correct fad has crept into show business whereby all performers in the theatrical world, regardless of gender, are known as 'actors'. Some male actors of the old school disapprove of this because they want to go to bed with actresses (whereas others are very happy, as they always have been, to go to bed with actors).

——

Laid-Back *Stand-Up*

A comedian who says four-letter words very slowly.

——

Lovable *TV Host*

There are no lovable TV hosts.

—

Mass Market *Original*

A book that is first published in paperback.

—

New *Classic*

A book or album that will be forgotten within six months.

—

New *Traditional*

A subgenre of music which tries to have it both ways.

———

Original *Copy*

A first edition of a book for which an exorbitant price may be demanded.

———

Reality TV *Star*

Reality TV is the invention of cheapskate television companies. Rather than spend money on actors and a script, they rely on the inevitable fact that, if you point a camera at an ordinary person long enough, he or she will do something stupid. The law of averages dictates that every now and then someone. of talent will emerge, but in very few cases do they merit the definition of 'star'.

Recorded *Live*

This expression is so commonly used in the music world that it's almost ceased to be an Oxymoron. It was also of course the title of a 1973 double LP by the group Ten Years After.

Shakespearean *Jokes*

Earnest teachers of English assure their students that the jokes in Shakespeare's plays were hilarious to the audiences of the time. We have no proof of this. But they sure as hell aren't funny now. Here's an example from that great seventeenth-century stand-up, the Fool in King Lear:

'FOOL: Thou canst tell why one's nose stands I' the middle on's face?

LEAR: No.

FOOL: Why, to keep one's eyes of either side's nose; what a man cannot smell out, he may spy into.'

One would say, 'Don't give up the day job', but for the fact that being a Fool was his day job.

———

Soft *Rock*

Music suitable for lifts and hotel foyers.

——

True *Story*

A movie whose credits include the words 'Based on a True Story' is guaranteed to diverge completely from the True Story on which it is based.

——

And of course, another very popular leisure activity is going out to eat, where restaurant menus can frequently provide a rich variety of Oxymorons:

MENU FOR THE ANNUAL DINNER OF THE OXYMORON SOCIETY

CANAPÉS
Outstanding Range of Dips, Finger Sandwiches and Elegant Crudités

---

FIRST COURSE
Jumbo Shrimp Cocktail

or

Line-Caught Scallops

or

Responsibly Farmed Foie Gras

MAIN COURSE
Boneless Ribs,
garnished with Fresh Prunes

or

T-Bone Fillet Steak
with Trimmed Mangetouts

or

Buffalo Wings
with Warm Salad and Mild Peppers

———

DESSERTS
Diet Ice Cream
with White Chocolate Brownies
or
Ugli Fruit Parfait
or
Our International Selection
of Local Cheeses

———

WINES
Soviet Champagne
Black Tower White Wine
Chateau Downunda

Hotel Coffee and
London's Finest Belgian Chocolates

10 Rela

Uncomplicated

tionships

Relationships are fragile things, and human beings have a unique capacity for screwing them up. However much they may try to forget the fact, everyone has parents, and that's often where the trouble starts. Siblings can complicate matters too. And then you grow up to the even more difficult task of venturing outside the family circle to form your own adult relationships. This is where things get really confusing. The business of dating has always been tricky, and it's doubtful whether modern technology – websites and social media – have made things any less complicated. Advances in what is acceptable in relationships – civil partnerships, same-sex marriage – are to be welcomed as definite progress. But the basic business of finding someone with whom you want to spend the rest of your life – and equally important, who wants to spend the rest of their life with you – doesn't seem to have got any easier.

Given the high emotional stakes and the conflicts created by passion, it is no surprise that relationships breed Oxymorons.

Adult *Male*

When it comes to relationships, there is no such thing as an Adult Male.

—

Amicable *Divorce*

If you believe such a thing exists, you should start one half of a divorced couple talking about the other. This will cure you of your illusion (assuming, of course, that you have three hours to spare).

—

Brotherly *Love*

Not always guaranteed – *cf.* Cain and Abel.

—

Casual *Sex*

See Free Love.

Free *Love*

A mythical ambition. It is very rare for both participants to be equally uninvolved. There will always come a point when one becomes more emotionally interested than the other and someone will get hurt.

Fun-Loving *Divorcee*

This usually refers to someone who, after the divorce, takes to the bottle.

Holy *Matrimony*

The use of ecclesiastical premises by people who never go to church under normal circumstances, but would like to have their wedding photos taken outside one.

―

Life-Time *Partner*

When men on dating sites claim they are looking for this, what they really mean is sex.

―

Long-Term *Relationship*

When men on dating sites claim they are looking for this, what they really mean is sex.

———

Love of my *Life*

When men on dating sites claim they are looking for this, what they really mean is sex.

———

Married *Life*

It is an observation as old as the institution itself that marriage puts an end to life enjoyed by the unattached. As the old Jewish joke puts it:

Q *Are you married?*
A *No, I've always been round-shouldered.*

—

Meaningful *One-Night Stand*

Huh, who are you trying to convince?

—

Merry *Widow*

See Fun-Loving Divorcee.

—

New *Position*

There is no such thing as a new position. People have 143
been having sex for so long that every position has
been used (but that needn't deprive you of the fun of
trying to find a new one).

—

'No Strings' *Sex*

See Free Love.

—

Open *Marriage*

When men say they want to have an 'open marriage', they mean they want to have sex with other women, without sacrificing the security of the wife waiting at home. They rarely want their women to play by the same rules. An open marriage is a bit like an open mind...or indeed an open skip...people are going to throw a lot of rubbish into it.

———

Open *Secret*

There are many of these in relationships, the most common being a husband having an affair that everyone knows about (except his wife).

———

Party *Animal*

Someone who describes themselves as this on a dating site will be loud, with a drink problem.

──────

Perfect *Partner*

Men or women who are looking for this often come to the conclusion that such a thing does not exist. And the requirements of the two genders are very different. Experts in the field of matchmaking have discovered that, while men's wish-lists are concerned with physical characteristics – height, shape, hair colour – women specify character traits – sensitivity, empathy and the inevitable GSOH. Is it any surprise that so many dates end in disaster?

──────

Personal *Space*

This is very difficult to attain within a relationship, but the expression is much used, especially by men. When a man says to his girlfriend, 'I think we'd better cool it a bit. I need some space', he means he wants to sleep with (or is already sleeping with) another woman.

———

Platonic *Relationship*

Such relationships do not exist. When a man and a woman spend time together, even if it is not physically expressed, there is always a sexual element present.

———

Prenuptial *Agreement*

This is rare. Few couples get through their
engagement without some disagreements.
Prenuptial Agreement is, however, not as rare as
Postnuptial Agreement.

____

Pure *Filth*

Pornography.

____

Purely *Physical*

If sex is purely physical, then one of you is doing something wrong.

———

Romantic *Pornography*

Though this is marketed as a subgenre, there is no romance in any pornography.

———

Safe *Sex*

Sex is never really safe because emotions tend to get involved.

———

Serially *Monogamous*

Used to describe someone who doesn't break off a relationship until he or she has got the next partner securely in place.

———

Tough *But Sensitive*

How weak insensitive men describe themselves on dating websites.

———

Acknowledgements

There are so many people without whose outgoing input *Seriously Funny* would not have made it into actual print. First, I would like to thank the midwife who helped me out at St Herod's Nursing Home. Then my parents whose untutored learning and disinterested enthusiasm for literature communicated itself to me. And I wouldn't have become a writer without my charismatic schoolteachers and the qualified encouragement I received from the academic fraternity at the Abergavenny University of Wales English Department.

I'd like to thank the people – Nigel Whitwham, Nigel Potts, Nigel Lenthall and Nigel Khrishnamurti – with whom, during my very constructive gap year, I shared a wakeful dormitory in that very smart backpackers' hotel in Kerala, where the fully formed embryonic idea for *Seriously Funny* was born.

I would like to say how much stimulus I got from the community of individuals on the MA creative writing course at AUE – particularly Armando Montez, Biff Runcorn, Salvia Carloponti, Miggy Truehorn and Seth Waterford – who read and generously critiqued my early finished drafts.

And I'd like to express my gratitude to the De Seet Trust, whose grant bought me time to complete the printed manuscript. Also, to the resident staff at Llangoghpogh Castle, the advanced writers' retreat where I more or less finished it.

It's vaguely obvious that I couldn't have written this book without the forward-looking backing of Suki, whose intermittently constant presence and counterintuitive objectivity enabled me to bring an expansive focus to the task in hand. I owe Suki for many timeless moments. Thanks to her too for the spontaneous regularity of caffeine infusions from her economical Nespresso machine!

And, last of all, I'd like to thank me, who actually wrote the bloody book.